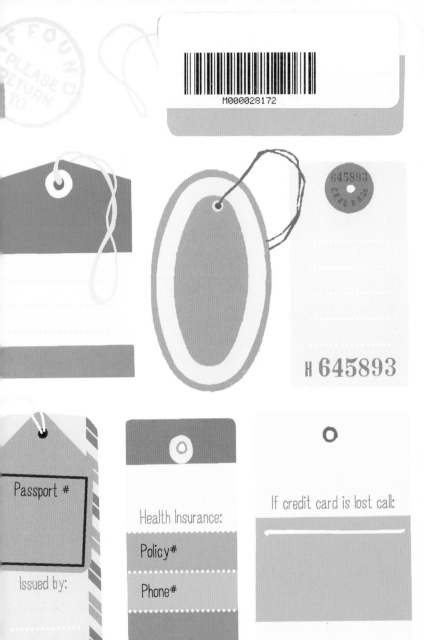

TO RESEARCH:

- [ ] ....
- [ ] ....
- [ ] ....
- [ ] ....
- [ ] ....
- [ ] ....
- [ ] ....
- [ ] ....
- [ ] ....
- [ ] ....
- [ ] ....
- [ ] ....
- [ ] ....
- [ ] ....
- [ ] ....
- [ ] ....
- [ ] ....
- [ ] ....
- [ ] ....
- [ ] ....
- [ ] ....
- [ ] ....
- [ ] ....

☐ ....
☐ ....
☐ ....
☐ ....
☐ ....
☐ ....
☐ ....
☐ ....
☐ ....
☐ ....
☐ ....
☐ ....
☐ ....
☐ ....
☐ ....
☐ ....
☐ ....
☐ ....
☐ ....
☐ ....
☐ ....
☐ ....

WAKE UP
LET'S:GO

DON'T FORGET:

- [ ]
- [ ]
- [ ]
- [ ]
- [ ]
- [ ]
- [ ]
- [ ]
- [ ]
- [ ]
- [ ]
- [ ]
- [ ]
- [ ]
- [ ]
- [ ]
- [ ]
- [ ]
- [ ]
- [ ]
- [ ]
- [ ]
- [ ]

GOING TO NEED:

- [ ] ....
- [ ] ....
- [ ] ....
- [ ] ....
- [ ] ....
- [ ] ....
- [ ] ....
- [ ] ....
- [ ] ....
- [ ] ....
- [ ] ....
- [ ] ....
- [ ] ....
- [ ] ....
- [ ] ....
- [ ] ....
- [ ] ....
- [ ] ....
- [ ] ....
- [ ] ....

FOR HIRE

BUSY

OFF DUTY

危险有电
DANGER! ENERGIZE

BD-FB箱

VIA AIR MAIL

NOTHING BEATS
FLYING AT SUNSET

Today:

Today:

Today:

Today:

Today:

Today:

Today:

Today:

Today:

Today:

Today:

Today:

CAFFE'
Pericaff
ROMA

TORREFAZIONE
TIBURTINA s.r.l.
Via Teodorico, 30/40
Tel. 06/44291212 r.a.

太古 taikoo

纯正白砂糖
premium white sugar

prima **2T** sugar

WELCOM
VIR
ISLA

Malongo

pure cane sugar

Miramar
HOTEL-RESORT
SANTA BARBARA

KABA
FINOMÍTOTT
KRISTÁLYCUKOR
5 g
M0Z 3071
ENERGIA TARTALMA:
1653 kjoule/100 g

AZUCAR

buen día...

Sucre blanc
5 GRS.

ZAXAPH
ΚΑΘ. ΒΑΡ. 9 ΓΡΑΜ.
καφές

BRAZITA
BRAZITA

CAFETEX ABEE

SUGAR
NET WEIGHT 9 GRAM.
καφές

· τupinamba

EIN GEV

SA
sug
Refined and pa
Malmö, Swe

Kandi
export-import
VELKOOBCHOD
Palackého 200
CHRUDIM
Tel : 0455/2122
Fax: 0455/2122

Kandi
export-import
VELKOOBCHOD

Sug

de watersport

sugar

rown
ar **apostrophe**

Zucker
Sugar
Sucre

KRAFT GMBH 8998 LINDENBERG
BR DEUTSCHLAND

AIRLAN
LANKA AI
A AIRSUG
LANKA
AIRLANKA
KA AIRL
LAN

BAGGAGE TO:

ATH

91-60 90 81

HOMEMADE CAR COVERS IN CAIRO

BAGGAGE STRAP TAG

CATHAY PACIFIC AIRWAYS

To

MANILA

MNL

FLIGHT No.

PASSENGER'S NAME

CX   62181

BRAZIL
(...ple-ish)

PUERTO RICO
(like drinking wheat toast)

ENGLAND
(black currant)

INDIA
(bitter cola)

TAIWAN
(muted apple)

KOREA
(...ke drinking
Red gum)

CUBA
(pineapple fizz)

IRELAND
(sour with
fruit bits)

EGYPT
(malted apple
with a pull-tab top)

PAKISTAN
(lime cream soda)

TRINIDAD
(...eed to chew)

JAPAN
(salty citrus
ion supply drink)

GHANA
(sweet maple flavor)

ITALY
(bitter herbal
Amaro)

MEXICO
(named after the
football team)

↑ 检票乘车
CHECK IN

← 小件寄存处
THE SMALL THING IS QUIC

→ 重点旅客候车处
VIP WAITING ROOM

PAR AVION

航 空 郵 便

PROHIBITED OUTFITS

INDIAN
HOLI POWDER

BAGGAGE TAG swiss

TO ZRH

FLG. NO 81-90

T-67 REV. 2-58 00865   SWISS

416042

Édition des Musées Nationaux
ENTRÉE T.R. 27 F

RÉUNION
DES MUSÉES NATIONAUX
—
ENTRÉE
TARIF RÉDUIT
27 F

416042

N°232   A018

RATP   CARNET **2** CL

SECTION URBAINE
Ⓜ BUS RER Ⓣ

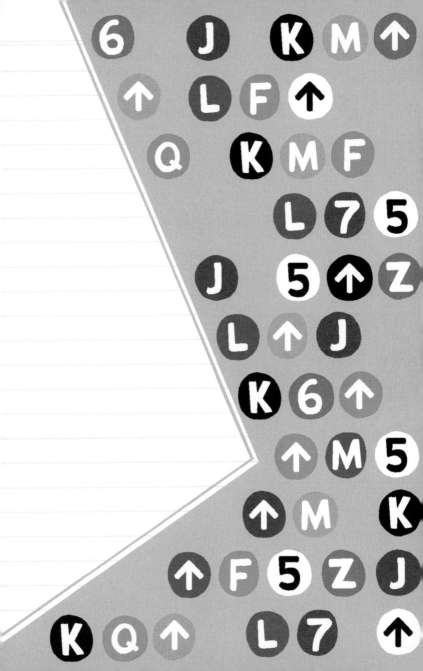

JAPANESE MOCHI
WITH A FRESH
STRAWBERRY
INSIDE

PLUGS

NORTH AMERICA,
JAPAN, TAIWAN
& BRAZIL

EUROPE

DENMARK

ISRAEL

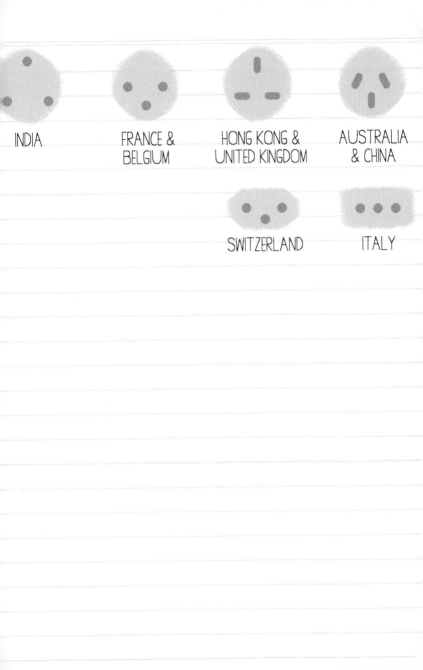

INDIA

FRANCE &
BELGIUM

HONG KONG &
UNITED KINGDOM

AUSTRALIA
& CHINA

SWITZERLAND

ITALY

ARE WE THERE YET?

IAD

DULLES INTERNATIONAL
AIRPORT

RAK

MARRAKECH-MENARA
AIRPORT

THS

SUKHOTHAI
AIRPORT

MAD

MADRID-BARAJAS
AIRPORT

MVD

MONTEVIDEO CARRASCO
AIRPORT

ICN

SEOUL INCHEON
AIRPORT

DEN

DENVER INTERNATIONAL
AIRPORT

LYS

LYON SAINT-EXUPÉRY
AIRPORT

PICKLED
MUD FISH

SOY SAUCE

BALLPARK
MUSTARD

KETCHUP

CURRY
KETCHUP

HERB
OLIVE

LT
GAR

WASABI

CHILI
OIL

MANGO
PICKLE

MARMITE

SALSA

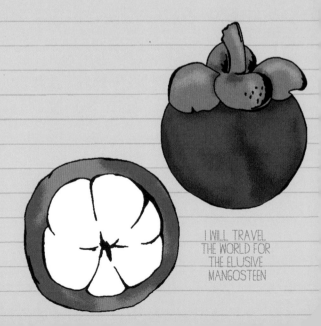

I WILL TRAVEL
THE WORLD FOR
THE ELUSIVE
MANGOSTEEN

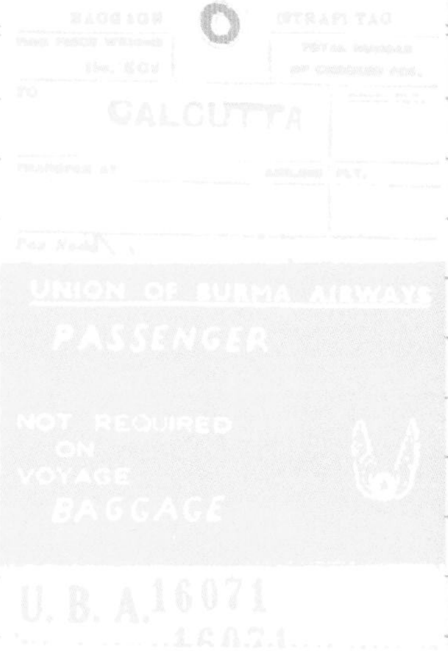

BAGGAGE STRAP TAG

TO CALCUTTA

TRANSFER AT   AIRLINE FLT.

Per Book

UNION OF BURMA AIRWAYS

PASSENGER

NOT REQUIRED
ON
VOYAGE
BAGGAGE

U. B. A. 16071
16071

MEHRAULI
FLOWER MARKET
BUNDLES

AIR PAR AVION MAIL

VARIOUS INTERNATIONAL COFFEE & TEA TRADITIONS

VIETNAMESE
COFFEE
(with condensed milk)

MAYAN COFFEE
(cinnamon, cayenne,
cocoa & cream)

ARABIC
COFFEE
(with cardamom)

ITALIAN
ESPRESSO
(drink quickly)

NEW YORK
ICED COFFEE
(giant sized in the
summer time)

NEW ORLEANS
COFFEE
(chicory)

CHILEAN HELADO
(chantily cream,
dulce de leche &
ground almonds)

PORTLAND
CAPPUCCINO
(fancy pants
artisanal)

INDONESIAN COFFEE
(with soda &
sweetened
condensed milk)

YEMENESE COFFEE
(with ginger)

CANADIAN COFFEE
(always fresh)

AUSTRALIAN
SWEET MILK COFFEE
(milk only, no water)

THAI ICED TEA
(with tamarind &
condensed milk,
served in a
plastic bag)

TURKISH CAY
(drink with a sugar
cube behind your teeth)

JAPANESE
MATCHA
(powdered
green tea)

TIBETAN PO CHA
(smokey black tea,
salt, yak butter & milk)

KENTUCKY
SWEET TEA
(with a lot of ice)

TAIWANESE BOBA
(flavored milk tea
with tapioca &
a huge, fat straw)

BRITISH TEA
(black tea with
cream & sugar)

RUSSIAN TEA
(served in a
podstakannik)

ARGENTINIAN
YERBA MATE
(will keep you up)

MOROCCAN TEA
(green tea with mint)

HONG KONG
LEMON TEA
(muddle the lemon)

KOREAN ROASTED
BARLEY TEA
(hot or iced)

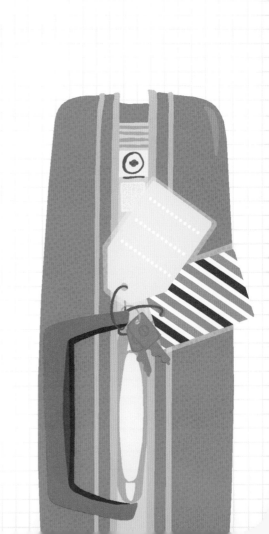

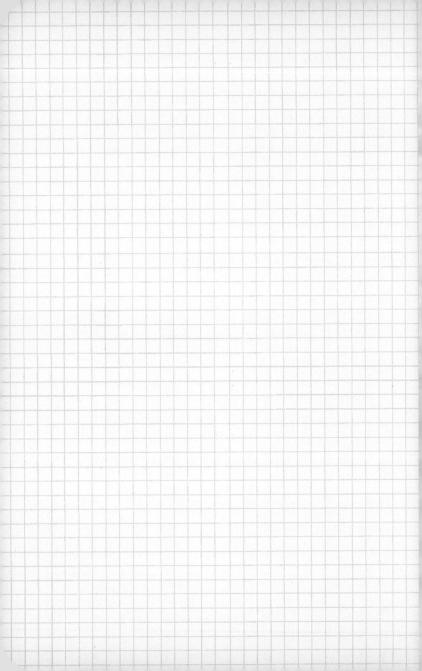

COLECTIVO

10 Cts.

1

Serie 2

2541

ENTREGUESE CADA
VEZ QUE SE SOLICI
TE O PAGARA NUE
VAMENTE EL VIAJE

45596

NORWICH

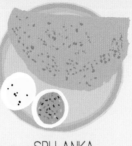

SRI LANKA

TEHRAN

KOMIŽA

CHIANG MAI

HANOI

NEW ORLEANS

SAN SALVADOR

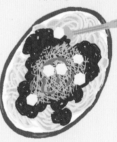

CINCINNATI

MOSCOW

SHANGHAI

PARIS

NO
SMOKING

NO EATING
OR DRINKING

NO FLAMMABLE
GOODS

NO
DURIANS

4/15 MARRAKECH

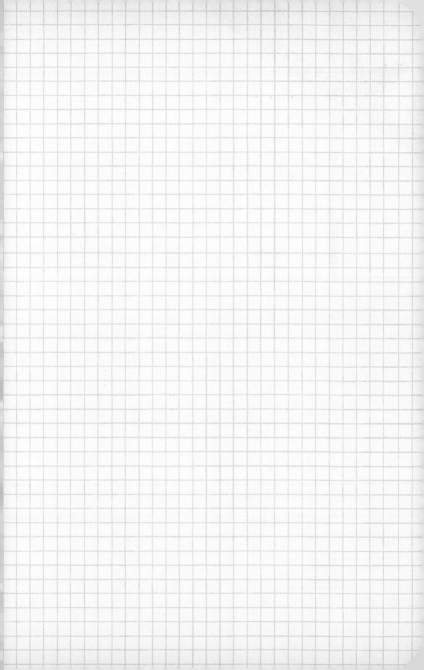

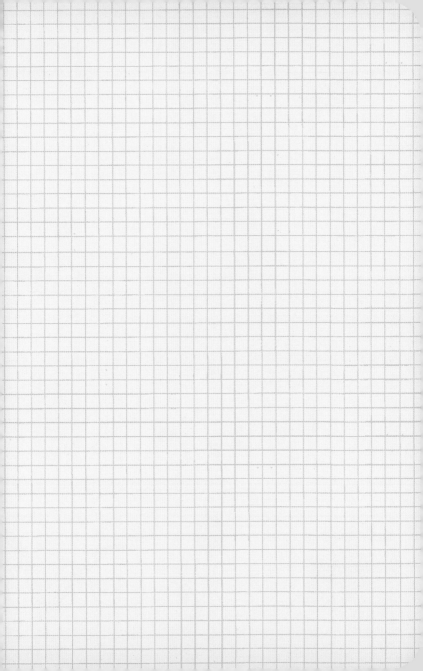

BANGKOK

SPOKANE

BALI

PROVENCE

SAN FRANCISCO

SICILY

HOKKAIDO

CLARKSDALE

GUANAJUATO

ANDALUCIA

HOLLAND

PUYO

CHINESE HEAD
MASSAGE &
EAR CLEANING

CLEAN SHAVE AT
THE NEIGHBORHOOD
BARBER

VENIK FOR A
RUSSIAN BATH

ICELANDIC
GEOTHERMAL
SALTWATER
SOAK

HEATED MARBLE
IN THE TURKISH BATH

BAGGAGE   TAG

شركة الطيران العربية المتحدة

UNITED ARAB AIRLINES

CAI

القاهرة

MS   139388

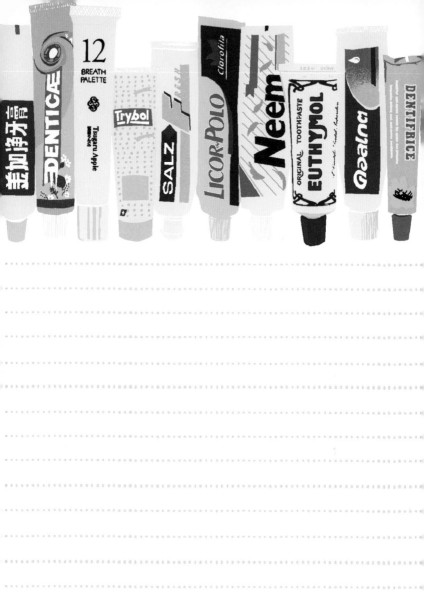

YU WAN:
FISHBALLS
(Hong Kong)

STINKY
TOFU
(Taiwan)

SLICED MANGO,
CHILI & LIME
(Los Angeles)

TAKOYAKI:
OCTOPUS DUMPLING
(Japan)

PALETA:
FRESH FRUIT ICE POP
(Mexico)

EGG CUSTARD
IN SHELL
(Laos)

KAMOTE-QU
CARMELIZED
SWEET POTAT
(Philippines)

CHEESE FONDUE
& BREAD
(Switzerland)

LAMB
KEBAB
(Istanbul)

CANDY
APPLE
(Jersey Shore)

CORN DOG
& DELI MUSTARD
(Coney Island)

GLAZED HAW BERRIES
& KUMQUATS
(Shanghai)

VARIOUS
SNACKS
ON STICKS

GRILLED C
CHILI & QU
(Cuba)

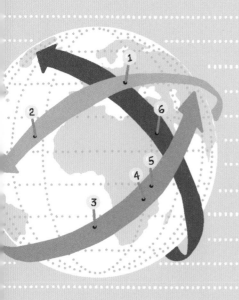

AÉROGRAMME

6 p.m. BERLIN

5 p.m. LONDON

1 a.m. SHANGHAI

8 p.m. MOSCOW

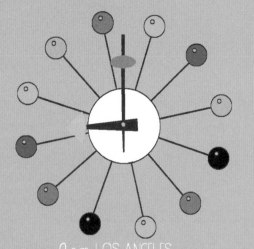

9 a.m. LOS ANGELES

9 p.m. DUBAI

12 a.m. HANOI

0:30 p.m. NEW DEHLI

2 p.m. BUENOS AIRES

ANBUL

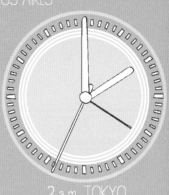

2 a.m. TOKYO

3 a.m. SYDNEY

VARIOUS METRO SYMBOLS

 AMSTERDAM

 ATHENS

 marta ATLANTA

 BALTIMORE

 BANGALORE

 BTS BANGKOK

 BRASILIA

GLASGOW

 BRUSSELS

 BUDAPEST

Subte BUENOS AIRES

 CAIRO

 CARACAS

 FORTALEZA

 GLASGOW

 GUADALAJARA

 HAIFA

 HANOVER

 HELSINKI

 KIEV

 KUALA LUMPUR

 LISBON

 LIVERPOOL

UNDERGROUND LONDON

 LOS ANGE

 MEXICO CITY

 MIAMI

 MINNEAPOLIS

 MINSK

 MONTREAL

 MOSCOW

 PHILADELPHIA

 PORTLAND

 PRAGUE

 RIO DE JANEIRO

 ROME

 ROTTERD

SINGAPORE

ST. LOUIS

STOCKHOLM

ST. PETERSBURG

CityRail SYDNEY

TAIPEI

BARCELONA   BEIJING   BERLIN   BILBAO   BOSTON

CHICAGO   CLEVELAND   COPENHAGEN   DALLAS   DELHI   DUBLIN

HIROSHIMA   HONG KONG   ICHEON   ISTANBUL   IZMIR

MADRID   MANILA   MARACAIBO   MARSEILLE   MEDELLÍN   MELBOURNE

NAGOYA   NEW JERSEY   NEW YORK   OSAKA   OSLO   PARIS

SALT LAKE   SAN FRANCISCO   SÃO PAULO   SEOUL   SF BAY AREA   SHANGHAI

TEHRAN   TOKYO   VIENNA   WARSAW   WASHINGTON

RULERS & CONVERSIONS

LENGTH
1 inch = 25.4 millimeters
1 inch = 2.54 centimeters
1 inch = 0.025 meters
1 foot = 12 inches
1 foot = 0.3 meters
1 yard = 3 feet
1 yard = 0.91 meters
1 mile = 1.61 kilometers

WEIGHT
1 pound = 16 ounces
1 pound = 453.59 grams
1 ounce = 28.35 grams
1 short ton = 2,000 pounds
1 short ton = 0.91 metric ton

SUPERLATIVE DESTINATIONS

RAINIEST SPOT
MOUNT WAI'ALE'ALE
Kaua'i, Hawaii
460–512 inches of rain per year

HIGHEST POINT
MOUNT EVEREST
Nepal/China
29,029 feet

DRIVE-IN
Shankweiler's
THEATRE

FASTEST ROLLER COASTER
FORMULA ROSSA
Ferrari World, Abu Dhabi, U.A.E.
150 mph

TALLEST WATERFALL
ANGEL FALLS
Venezuela
3,212 feet

CAPACITY

1 ounce = 29.57 milliliters
1 cup = 236.59 milliliters
1 pint = 16 ounces
1 pint = 2 cups
1 quart = 2 pints
1 gallon = 4 quarts

AREA

1 sq. foot = 144 sq. inches
1 sq. foot = 0.09 sq. meters
1 sq. yard = 9 sq. feet
1 acre = 4840 sq. yards
1 sq. mile = 640 acres

LONGEST RIVER
NILE
Egypt, Africa
4,132 miles

DRIEST PLACE
ATACAMA DESERT
Chile
rain has never been recorded

OLDEST DRIVE-IN MOVIE THEATER
SHANKWEILER'S
Orefield, Pennsylvania
continuous operation since 1934

HIGHEST HUMAN HABITATION
LA RINCONADA
Peru
16,732 feet

LONGEST FESTIVAL
NADUN FESTIVAL
Northwest China's Qinghai Province
63-day celebration of the wheat harvest

A BIT OF TRANSLATION

ENGLISH	FRENCH	SPANISH	GERMAN
Hello	Bonjour	Hola	Hallo
Goodbye	Au revoir	Adios	Auf wiederse
Yes	Oui	Sí	Ja
No	Non	No	Nein
Please	S'il vous plaît	Por favor	Bitte
Thank you	Merci	Gracias	Danke
You're welcome	De rien	De nada	Bitte
Excuse me	Excusez-moi	Perdón	Entschuldigung
My name is	Je m'appelle	Me llamo	Mein name ist
How much?	Combien?	Cuánto?	Wie viel?
Where is	Où est	Dónde está	Wo ist
The toilet	La toilette	El baño	Die Toilette
A room	Une chambre	Un cuarto	Ein zimmer

SOME PICTORIAL SIGN LANGUAGE

ESSENTIALS

TRANSPORT

JAPANESE	MANDARIN	ITALIAN	HINDI
nnichiwa	Ni hao	Buon giorno	Namaste
yōnara	Zaijian	Arrivederci	Alavida
	Dui	Sì	Hām
shi	Bu	No	Nahim
Kudasai	Qing	Per favore	Kripaya
no arigato	Xie xie	Grazie	Dhanyavaad
tashimashite	Bu ke qi	Prego	Apaka svagata hai
mimasen	Duibuqi	Scusi	Maaf keejie
tashi wa	Wo shi	Mi chiamo	Mera nama hai
nogurai?	Duo shao?	Quanto?	Kitana?
ko ni aru	Zai nali	Dove è	Kaham hai
re	Cesuo	Il gabinetto	Saucalaya
va	Yi shi	Una camera	Eka kamara

BUONGIORNO
KONICHIWA
HI

Copyright © 2013 by Kate Pocrass

All rights reseved. No part of this book may
be reproduced in any form without written
permission from the publisher.

ISBN:
978-1-4521-1193-3

Manufactured
in China

Designed by Kate Pocrass

See the full
range of
Kate Pocrass
gift and
stationery
products at:

www.chroniclebooks.com

CHRONICLE BOO
680 SECOND STREET
SAN FRANCISCO, CA 941
WWW.CHRONICLEBOOKS.C

10 9 8 7 6 5 4 3 2